MALAWI 2016 HUMAN RIGHTS REPORT

EXECUTIVE SUMMARY

Malawi is a multiparty democracy. Constitutional power is shared between the president and the 193 National Assembly members. The 2014 elections for president, parliament, and local councils were characterized by international observers as free, transparent, and credible.

Civilian authorities maintained effective control over the security forces.

The most significant human rights problems in the country included unlawful police killings; excessive use of force, including torture by security officers; and sexual exploitation of children, including early and forced marriage.

Other human rights problems included arbitrary arrest and detention; harsh prison and detention center conditions; lengthy pretrial detention; mob violence; societal discrimination and violence against women; harmful traditional practices, including sexual initiation rituals; trafficking in persons; discrimination against lesbian, gay, bisexual, transgender, and intersex (LGBTI) persons; discrimination against persons with disabilities; violence against persons with albinism; and child labor.

In some cases the government took steps to prosecute officials who committed abuses, but impunity remained a problem.

Section 1. Respect for the Integrity of the Person, Including Freedom from:

a. Arbitrary Deprivation of Life and other Unlawful or Politically Motivated Killings

There were isolated reports the government or its agents committed arbitrary or unlawful killings.

Police arbitrarily shot and sometimes killed suspected criminals. There were several reported cases similar to the following example. On March 30, police shot and killed a fleeing robbery suspect in Ndirande, Blantyre.

Perpetrators of past abuses were occasionally punished, but investigations often were delayed, abandoned, or remained inconclusive. On October 5, the High

Court convicted Police Constable Stewart Lobo of the 2011 murder of a protester during antigovernment demonstrations. Eight other officers arrested in connection with the incident remained free on bail awaiting trial at year's end. On August 24, the government paid compensation of 31 million Malawian kwacha (MWK) ($42,900) to the families of 10 persons killed during the demonstrations.

b. Disappearance

There were no reports of politically motivated disappearances.

c. Torture and Other Cruel, Inhuman, or Degrading Treatment or Punishment

The constitution and law prohibit such practices; however, police sometimes used excessive force and other unlawful practices. For example, on July 10, community members in Mpemba, Blantyre, protested the severe beating of Piyasoni Magombo inflicted by police during his arrest. Magombo died from injuries sustained during the beating. The Malawi Human Rights Commission (MHRC) stated in its annual report that torture was widespread in prisons.

Prison and Detention Center Conditions

Prison and detention center conditions remained harsh and potentially life threatening due to overcrowding and poor sanitation; inadequate food, potable water, heating, ventilation, lighting, and health care; and torture.

The MHRC and nongovernmental organizations (NGOs) working in prisons expressed concern regarding the human rights of detained persons. During the year the MHRC released a report that cited overcrowding, poor sanitation, and inadequate food and health care as major problems in prisons and detention centers. It stated that torture was widespread and most prisoners and detainees lived in degrading and inhuman conditions. From January to August, the MHRC received two complaints regarding the rights of prisoners and other detainees. It received four such complaints in 2015. The low number of submitted complaints was believed to be due to fear of retaliation by authorities.

Physical Conditions: According to the Inspectorate of Prisons, the government remained largely noncompliant with the High Court's 2009 requirement to improve prison conditions. A 2014 inspection tour that covered 90 percent of prisons found recurrent problems of poor sanitation, poor diet, overcrowding, prisoner abuse, poor ventilation, detention without charge beyond 48 hours, understaffing, prison staff corruption, and insufficient prisoner rehabilitation such as education and vocational training.

Overcrowding and malnutrition remained problems. On September 6, the Malawi Prison Services reported the total prison population was 14,018, more than double prison capacity of 7,000. Police held detainees in police stations for long periods beyond the legal limit of 48 hours, which led to pervasive cell overcrowding.

Authorities held women separately from men but often held pretrial detainees and convicted prisoners together. In police detention children were not always held separately from adults. Although inadequate, detention facilities for women and children were generally better than men's facilities. Several hundred irregular migrants as young as 13 were held with the general prison population even after their immigration-related sentences had been served.

As of September, according to the prison service 77 inmates died in prison. Leading causes of death were tuberculosis (24 inmates), malaria (nine inmates), anemia (seven inmates), and AIDS (five).

Basic emergency medical care generally was available in the daytime but unavailable after regular working hours. Daily prison rations were meager. Officials allowed family members to provide food and encouraged inmates to grow vegetables and raise livestock in rural prisons. Malnutrition in the prison population remained a problem, however, particularly in urban prisons.

Inadequate infrastructure remained a serious problem. Prisons and detention centers had no provisions for temperature control other than wood fires.

Administration: Recordkeeping was inadequate. Each prison had a designated welfare officer, some of whom had received specialized training, to receive prisoner complaints regarding conditions. The complaints process, however, was primarily verbal and informal, allowed for censorship, and provided little follow-up. The MHRC received only two complaints during the year. Prisoners sometimes had the opportunity to complain to NGOs that recorded cases for inclusion in government advocacy and reports, but this rarely resulted in follow-up on individual cases.

Independent Monitoring: During the year the government permitted domestic and international NGOs and the media to visit and monitor prison conditions and donate basic supplies. Domestic NGOs, the Malawi Red Cross Society, and diplomatic representatives had unrestricted access to prisons.

d. Arbitrary Arrest or Detention

The constitution and law prohibit arbitrary arrest and detention; however, the government did not always observe these prohibitions.

Role of the Police and Security Apparatus

The government exercised effective control over the Malawi Defense Force (MDF) and Malawi Police Service (MPS). The MPS, under the Ministry of Home Affairs, has responsibility for law enforcement and maintenance of order. The MDF has responsibility for external security. The MDF was sometimes asked to carry out policing activity. The MDF commander reports directly to the president as commander in chief.

Police were inefficient, poorly trained, and corrupt (see section 4). Impunity was a problem. Officers suspected of misconduct generally were transferred rather than investigated, and disciplined if found guilty. Authorities, however, prosecuted officers accused of involvement in serious crimes such as robbery, murder, or rape (see section 1.a.).

Like other elements of government, the MDF and MPS were subject to investigation for corruption. In July 2015 the Anti-Corruption Bureau (ACB) arrested former army chief General Henry Odillo and his former deputy, Lieutenant Colonel Clement Kafuwa, on corruption charges in connection with contracts for military equipment that was never delivered. The two were arraigned at the High Court and released on bail. The trial began in October but had yet to conclude by year's end.

The MDF and MPS cooperated with corruption investigations by the ACB but did not carry out their own internal investigations. Government mechanisms to investigate and punish abuse and corruption were only marginally effective due in large part to funding and human resource constraints.

The inspector general of police remained committed to the professionalization of the MPS. The Professional Responsibility Unit (previously known as the Internal Affairs Department) of the MPS investigates police misconduct, including whether killings or other misconduct that occurred in the line of duty were justifiable.

Police continued to train officers on internal investigations, victims' rights, sexual abuse, domestic violence, and trafficking in persons. Police continued to receive foreign assistance for training and equipment.

Arrest Procedures and Treatment of Detainees

The law provides an accused person the right to challenge the legality of detention, have access to legal counsel, and be released from detention or informed of charges by a court within 48 hours of arrest; however, authorities often ignored these rights. Police apprehended most suspects without a warrant if they had reasonable grounds to believe a crime was being or had been committed. Only in cases involving corruption or white-collar crime were arrest warrants normally issued by a duly authorized official based on evidence presented. The use of temporary remand warrants to circumvent the 48-hour rule was widespread. Police frequently demanded bribes to authorize bail, which was often granted to reduce overcrowding in jails, rather than on the merits of a case. Relatives were sometimes denied access to detainees. There were no reports detainees were held incommunicado or held under house arrest.

Detainees who could afford counsel were able to meet with counsel in a timely manner. While the government is obligated by law to provide legal services to indigent detainees, such aid was provided almost exclusively to suspects charged with homicide. In March 2015 the Legal Aid Bureau replaced the Department of Legal Aid as the institution mandated to provide legal assistance to indigent persons. Underfunded and having only nine lawyers, the bureau could not provide timely legal assistance to the indigent, and sometimes none at all. It concentrated on assisting prisoners in processing bail and appeal applications.

The Center for Legal Assistance and the Paralegal Advisory Service Institute, NGOs that assist prisoners with legal matters, provided limited free legal assistance to expedite the trials of detainees. Priority was given to the sick, the young, mothers with infants, persons with disabilities, and those in extended pretrial detention.

Arbitrary Arrest: The constitution and law prohibit arbitrary arrest, unlawful detention, or false arrest. Authorities, however, made arbitrary arrests based on sections of the penal code pertaining to rogues and vagabonds, conduct likely to cause breach of peace, and obstruction of police officers. Although prostitution is legal, police regularly harassed sex workers. For example, on February 24, 19 sex workers in Dedza were arrested, charged, and convicted of living off the proceeds of prostitution, an offense generally applied to prosecute pimps since the relevant statute refers to "proceeds of another person's performance of prostitution."

<u>Pretrial Detention</u>: Of the total prison population of 14,018 inmates, 2,275, or 16 percent, were in pretrial detention. Despite a statutory 90-day limit on pretrial detention, authorities held most homicide suspects in pretrial detention for two to three years. There was evidence some homicide detainees remained in prison awaiting trial for much longer periods, but reliable information on the number and situation of these detainees was unavailable.

To reduce case backlog and excessive pretrial detention, certain cases were directed to local courts and "camp courts" organized by civil society groups. Camp courts expedite cases by bringing magistrates to prisons. Paralegals gather cases of pretrial detainees awaiting trial for excessive periods, who are held unlawfully, or who have been granted bail but are unable to meet the terms set by the court. Magistrates, along with the court clerk and police prosecutor, work through the list, granting bail to some, reducing bail for others, dismissing cases, or setting trial dates.

<u>Detainee's Ability to Challenge Lawfulness of Detention before a Court</u>: The law provides an accused person the right to challenge the legality of detention but does not provide for compensation if found to have been unlawfully detained. Lack of knowledge of statutes and of access to representation meant detainees did not challenge the legality of their detention.

e. Denial of Fair Public Trial

The constitution and law provide for an independent judiciary, and the government generally respected judicial independence. The judicial system, however, was inefficient and handicapped by serious weaknesses, including poor recordkeeping; a shortage of judges, attorneys, and other trained personnel; heavy caseloads; corruption; and lack of resources. The slow-moving judicial system, including extensive delays due to motion practice (a three-step court order request), a low bar for granting injunctions, judge shopping, prosecutorial delay tactics, frequent recusals, and lawyers and witnesses not being present on trial dates, undermined the government's ability to dispense justice.

The MDF conducts courts-martial but no military or security tribunals. Used more frequently than courts-martial is a nonjudicial procedure under which cases are dealt with summarily by senior officers without a formal trial process. In both procedures military personnel are entitled to the same rights as persons accused in civilian courts.

Trial Procedures

The constitution and law provide for the right to a fair public trial, and an independent judiciary generally enforced this right.

Defendants are presumed innocent. The constitution and law provide for an accused to be informed of charges by a court within 48 hours of arrest, with free interpretation if necessary. Defendants have the right to be present at their trial, to have an attorney, and, if indigent, an attorney provided at state expense, but such assistance was usually limited to homicide cases. Defendants have the right to challenge prosecution or plaintiff evidence and witnesses, present their own witnesses and evidence, and access government-held evidence relevant to their cases. By law they may not be compelled to testify or confess guilt. The law does not specify a given length of time for the accused to prepare a defense. The slow pace of trials affords defendants adequate time to prepare but not to adequate facilities due to insufficient prison system funding. The law extends the above rights to all persons. All persons have the right of appeal; however, appeals often were delayed for years and sometimes never addressed by the higher court.

The judiciary's budgetary and administrative problems led to backlogs that effectively denied expeditious trials for most defendants and kept some defendants in pretrial detention for long time periods. Recruitment and retention of government attorneys remained a problem. MPS prosecutors with limited legal training prosecuted the majority of criminal cases. The Directorate of Public Prosecutions in the Ministry of Justice customarily tried high-profile cases and those involving the most serious offenses. As of September the directorate had one prosecuting attorney supported by 18 paralegals, who also prosecuted certain lower court cases.

Political Prisoners and Detainees

There were no reports of political prisoners or detainees.

Civil Judicial Procedures and Remedies

There is an independent and impartial judiciary in civil matters, and citizens have access to a court to submit lawsuits seeking damages for, or cessation of, human rights violations. Individuals and organizations may appeal adverse domestic decisions to regional courts. The law provides for administrative and judicial remedies for alleged wrongs; however, a lack of legal professionals restricted the number of human rights cases pursued and resulted in a large backlog. As of August 31, there were 377 licensed legal practitioners. Through September the MHRC received 82 complaints of limited access to justice and eight complaints of unfair administrative justice procedures.

f. Arbitrary or Unlawful Interference with Privacy, Family, Home, or Correspondence

The constitution and law prohibit such actions, but the government did not always respect these prohibitions.

The law permits police officers of the rank of subinspector or higher to conduct searches without a court warrant if they have reasonable grounds for believing something needed for an investigation cannot otherwise be obtained without undue delay. Before conducting a search without a warrant, the officer must write reasonable-grounds justification and give a copy to the owner or occupant of the place to be searched.

Section 2. Respect for Civil Liberties, Including:

a. Freedom of Speech and Press

The constitution and law provide for freedom of speech and press, and the government generally respected these rights.

Freedom of Speech and Expression: Antisedition and breach of peace laws were sometimes used to stifle criticism. For example, on February 22 and 23, three opposition parliamentarians were arrested and charged with sedition for their statements in a social media conversation in which they discussed taking political advantage of public discontent with the government. They were released on bail following a brief detention.

Violence and Harassment: Authorities sometimes attempted to intimidate journalists who reported criticism of the ruling party. On June 17, the Malawi Communications Regulatory Authority (MACRA) summoned the host of a call-in program on Dziko FM to chastise him for failing to "control callers" who made remarks critical of the president and his government. In August, MACRA accused representatives of the Zodiak Broadcasting Corporation of "lacking journalistic judgement" for allowing opposition members of parliament "to make sensitive remarks without being directed or controlled."

<u>Censorship or Content Restrictions</u>: Journalists sometimes practiced self-censorship, especially at government-owned media outlets such as the Malawi Broadcasting Corporation (MBC) Radios One and Two and MBC TV.

Internet Freedom

The government did not restrict or disrupt access to the internet or censor online content, and there were no reports that the government monitored private online communications without appropriate legal authority. Lack of infrastructure and the high cost of internet connections limited internet access. According to the International Telecommunication Union, approximately 9.3 percent of the population used the internet in 2015.

Academic Freedom and Cultural Events

There were no government restrictions on academic freedom during the year; however, the government sporadically censored films that it deemed contained culturally sensitive or sexually explicit material.

The Malawi Censorship Board Secretariat is responsible for reviewing and classifying plays, films, and foreign music for adult content as well as regulating public theaters.

b. Freedom of Peaceful Assembly and Association

Freedom of Assembly

The constitution and law provide for freedom of assembly, but the government did not always respect this right. On September 21, 26 peacefully protesting students from Lilongwe University of Agriculture and Natural Resources were arrested and charged with conduct likely to breach the peace. They were subsequently released on bail. Their case was pending at year's end.

Freedom of Association

The constitution and law provide for the freedom of association, and the government generally respected this right. Nevertheless, the government required registration of all NGOs and political parties. NGOs must register with three different government entities and pay significant yearly registration fees.

c. Freedom of Religion

See the Department of State's *International Religious Freedom Report* at www.state.gov/religiousfreedomreport/.

d. Freedom of Movement, Internally Displaced Persons, Protection of Refugees, and Stateless Persons

The constitution and law provide for freedom of internal movement, foreign travel, emigration, and repatriation, and the government generally respected these rights.

The government cooperated with the UN High Commissioner for Refugees (UNHCR) and other humanitarian organizations in providing protection and assistance to refugees, asylum seekers, and other persons of concern. In March the government reopened the Luwani camp in the south to accommodate an influx of approximately 10,000 asylum seekers from Mozambique. As of August 18, UNHCR had transferred 1,919 of the asylum seekers to the Luwani camp, and the remaining 8,000 had returned to Mozambique. At year's end there were approximately 27,000 refugees at the Dzaleka camp in the north, with more refugees continuing to arrive, mostly from the Democratic Republic of the Congo and Burundi.

Abuse of Migrants, Refugees, and Stateless Persons: Security forces sometimes intimidated refugees and asylum seekers. Police routinely detained and returned refugees found outside the Dzaleka camp, including those with proper identity documents. Local citizens often accused refugees of committing various crimes.

In-country Movement: Refugees were subject to an encampment policy that restricted them to the Dzaleka and Luwani refugee camps, the only two officially designated refugee camps. Authorities periodically rounded up and returned those who left the camp.

Protection of Refugees

<u>Access to Asylum</u>: The law provides for the granting of asylum or refugee status, and as of August the government provided protection to approximately 29,000 individuals. Asylum seekers primarily came from the Great Lakes region of Africa and Mozambique.

There were multiple reports of so-called survival sex by refugees to obtain income to supplement food rations and other necessities in the camp. Gender-based violence and other criminal activities were reported in the camp.

From January to August, the MHRC received three complaints of mistreatment at the Dzaleka refugee camp.

<u>Employment</u>: In general the government did not allow refugees to seek employment or educational opportunities outside the camp. Most refugees were dependent on donor-funded food assistance. A small number of refugees with professional degrees, especially those with medical training, received permits to pursue employment and other opportunities outside the camp.

<u>Access to Basic Services</u>: UNHCR, NGOs, and the government collaborated to provide most basic services. Refugees had access to education and health-care services through camp schools and clinics. These overtaxed facilities served both refugees and local communities. A rapid increase in the refugee population and the inability of most refugees to grow food or earn money due to the encampment policy limited the available food and services to that provided by donors through UNHCR and the World Food Program. Ration allocations were below recommended levels due to insufficient funding.

While local laws and the justice system applied to refugees, access to the justice system was limited by inefficiencies and inadequate resources. With only 13 police officers assigned to the Dzaleka camp, law enforcement capacity was extremely limited.

<u>Temporary Protection</u>: The government provided temporary protection to individuals who may not qualify as refugees; however, no reliable statistics were available.

Section 3. Freedom to Participate in the Political Process

The constitution and law provide citizens the ability to choose their government through free and fair periodic elections held by secret ballot and based on universal and equal suffrage.

Elections and Political Participation

Recent Elections: In 2014 citizens voted in simultaneous presidential, parliamentary, and local elections. Voters elected Arthur Peter Mutharika of the Democratic Progressive Party as president with 36.4 percent of the vote. Mutharika defeated incumbent president Joyce Banda, marking the first time an incumbent party lost the presidency since the country's first multiparty election in 1994. Presidential and vice presidential debates took place and were broadcast on radio and television for the first time, which provided voters a new tool for evaluating and contrasting candidates and their policies.

International observers characterized the elections as generally peaceful, free, credible, and transparent, although there were shortcomings. During the pre-election period, President Banda and her People's Party dominated state media and used public resources for campaigning and patronage. Rumors of plans for election fraud were rife but largely unfounded. Public confidence in the election commission was tested when widespread errors in the voter rolls became known in 2014. That confidence was further undermined on election day when polling materials were not delivered on time to many polling stations, resulting in the extension of voting for one to two days at several stations. Trailing significantly in the polls according to early vote counts, President Banda attempted unconstitutionally to nullify the results and order new elections, alleging irregularities and fraud. The courts rejected this move, and vote counting proceeded. This and other election law rulings contributed to a peaceful and lawful presidential election. While localized irregularities existed in the polling, President Mutharika's nearly 450,000-vote margin of victory was decisive. Also in 2014 successful local elections filled the positions of local councilors following a nine-year gap; the term of councilors elected in 2000 expired in 2005.

Participation of Women and Minorities: Cultural and traditional gender bias and lower levels of literacy, education, and economic empowerment prevented women from participating in the political process to the same extent as men. There were 32 women in the 193-seat National Assembly and 56 women among the 462 elected local councilors. There were three women in the 20-member cabinet. Women constituted approximately 25 percent of the civil service. There were 10 female justices among the 34 Supreme Court of Appeal and High Court justices.

Section 4. Corruption and Lack of Transparency in Government

The law provides criminal penalties for conviction of corruption by officials, but the government did not implement the law effectively. Officials sometimes engaged in corrupt practices with impunity. There was little criminal or professional accountability for those involved.

The government, in cooperation with donors, continued implementation of an action plan to pursue cases of corruption, review how the "Cashgate" corruption scandal occurred, and introduce internal controls and improved systems to prevent further occurrences. Progress on investigations and promised reforms was slow. The vice president headed a public-sector reform effort to address the factors that allowed corruption to thrive.

<u>Corruption</u>: The investigation and prosecution of approximately 70 individuals, primarily mid-level civil servants arrested in 2013 for involvement in the theft of approximately 20 billion MWK ($55 million at the time) through fraudulent transactions--the Cashgate corruption scandal--proceeded slowly. As of September, 12 cases resulted in convictions with prison sentences ranging from three to 11 years. At year's end no high-level officials had been arrested or charged and prosecuted for Cashgate-related offenses. On May 5, the Anti-Corruption Bureau deputy director recused himself from serving as lead prosecutor on the state's corruption case against former president Bakili Muluzi, leaving only junior ACB lawyers available to prosecute the case. Muluzi had been on trial since 2006 for graft totaling eight billion MWK ($11 million).

<u>Financial Disclosure</u>: The constitution requires the president, vice president, and members of the cabinet to disclose their assets in writing to the speaker of the National Assembly within three months of being elected or appointed. There is no requirement in law for the speaker to make the declarations public or available to other members of parliament. The Public Officers Declaration of Assets Law requires officials in 48 categories, ranging from the president, members of parliament, and senior officials down to specific categories of civil servants, including traffic police and immigration officers, to make financial disclosures. Noncompliance is a basis for dismissal, and individuals who knowingly provide inaccurate information may be fined, dismissed, and imprisoned. The declarations are to be accessible to the public upon request, but the director has the authority to deny such requests. Denials may be appealed to the High Court. On October 4, the Directorate of Assets Declaration revealed that 28 members of parliament,

including some cabinet members, failed to declare their assets; however, no sanctions were announced.

<u>Public Access to Information</u>: The constitution provides for public access to government information but only insofar as such information is required for the exercise of an individual's rights. There were no reports of fees charged or denial of access to requested records. In the absence of implementing legislation, access to government information was rarely sought and poorly understood.

Section 5. Governmental Attitude Regarding International and Nongovernmental Investigation of Alleged Violations of Human Rights

A variety of domestic and international human rights groups generally operated without government restriction, training civic educators, advocating changes to existing laws and cultural practices, and investigating and publishing their findings on human rights cases. Government officials were somewhat cooperative and responsive to their views.

<u>Government Human Rights Bodies</u>: The MHRC, an independent government-chartered institution, is mandated by the constitution to promote and protect human rights and investigate violations of human rights. Despite its independent leadership, resource shortfalls resulted in a backlog of cases, delayed production of reports, and limited investigation of human rights violations. The MHRC received 324 complaints of human rights violations through August.

The Office of the Ombudsman is mandated to investigate government officials responsible for human rights violations and other abuses. The ombudsman does not take legal action against government officials but may order administrative action to redress grievances and may recommend prosecution to the director of public prosecution. The office had 15 investigators. During the year it launched a website with regular updates on its activities.

Section 6. Discrimination, Societal Abuses, and Trafficking in Persons

Women

<u>Rape and Domestic Violence</u>: The penal code criminalizes rape with a maximum penalty if convicted of death. The Marriage, Divorce, and Family Relations Act enacted in 2015 explicitly introduced the concept of spousal rape, but the act does not prescribe specific penalties and only applies to legally separated spouses.

Spousal rape may be prosecuted under the rape provisions of the penal code. The government generally enforced the law effectively, and convicted rapists routinely received prison sentences. Data on the prevalence of rape or spousal rape, prosecutions, and convictions were unavailable; however, press reporting of rape and defilement arrests and convictions were an almost daily occurrence. Although the maximum penalty for conviction of rape is death or life imprisonment, the courts generally imposed fixed prison sentences. For cases of conviction of indecent assault on women and girls, the maximum penalty is 14 years in prison.

The Ministry of Gender, Children, Disability, and Social Welfare conducted public education campaigns to combat domestic violence and rape.

The law provides a maximum penalty of life imprisonment for conviction of domestic violence and recognizes that both men and women may be perpetrators as well as victims. According to the *2012 Gender Based Violence Baseline Survey*, 40 percent of women experienced sexual violence and 30 percent experienced other physical violence. Domestic violence, especially wife beating, was common, although women seldom discussed the problem openly, and victims rarely sought legal recourse. Legal experts and human rights workers attributed victims' reluctance to report their abusers to economic dependence on the abuser, lack of awareness of their legal rights, and fear of retribution and ostracism. Police regularly investigated cases of rape and sexual assault but did not normally intervene in domestic disputes. Police support units provided shelter to some abuse victims and dealt with human rights and gender-based violence, but officers' capacity to assist and document cases was limited.

Female Genital Mutilation/Cutting (FGM/C): The law does not specifically prohibit FGM/C. According to press reports from 2011, some cases of FGM/C were prosecuted as unlawful wounding. A 2014 UN Human Rights Committee report expressed concern regarding the existence of FGM/C in some regions of the country. A few small ethnic groups practiced FGM/C. In most cases FGM/C was performed on girls between ages 10 and 15.

Other Harmful Traditional Practices: The Gender Equality Act of 2013 prohibits certain harmful traditional practices, including "widow cleansing" and "widow inheritance." Nonetheless, in a few isolated areas, widows were sometimes forced to have sex with male in-laws or a designee as part of a culturally mandated "sexual cleansing" ritual following the death of the husband. In some cases widows were "inherited" by a brother-in-law or other male relative. The government and NGOs continued efforts to abolish such practices by raising awareness concerning the inherent dangers of such behavior, including the risk of HIV/AIDS transmission.

"Kupimbira," a practice that allows a poor family to receive a loan or livestock in exchange for daughters of any age, existed in some areas.

Despite certain legal prohibitions, many abusive practices, including the secret initiation of girls into the socially prescribed roles of womanhood, continued. Such initiations were often aimed at preparing girls for marriage with emphasis on training girls how to engage in sexual acts. In a few traditional communities, girls as young as age 10 were forced to have sexual relations with older men as part of such initiation rites. According to UN estimates, one in 10 citizens is infected with HIV, and this practice places girls at great risk of infection. On July 25, in response to negative publicity from the BBC and other international news media, the president ordered the arrest of Eric Aniva for having sex with children. An HIV-positive man, Aniva reportedly was paid to have sex with girls as part of initiation rites but failed to disclose his condition to the families that hired him. He was tried and convicted on two counts of engaging in harmful cultural practices and sentenced to two years' imprisonment. In September police and traditional leaders burned initiation camps in Mangochi District where girls were instructed on sex and sometimes lost their virginity.

Sexual Harassment: The Gender Equality Act makes sexual harassment punishable if convicted of up to five years' imprisonment. Extreme cases could be prosecuted under certain sections of the penal code, such as indecent assault on a woman or girl, which provides for up to a 14-year prison sentence if convicted, or insulting the modesty of a woman, a misdemeanor punishable by one year's incarceration if convicted. Although sexual harassment was believed to be widespread, there were no data on its prevalence or on the effectiveness of government enforcement of the law.

Reproductive Rights: The government recognized the right of couples and individuals to decide the number, spacing, and timing of their children; manage their reproductive health; and have access to the information and means to do so, free from discrimination, coercion, or violence. The government allowed health-care clinics and local NGOs to operate freely in disseminating information on family planning under the guidance of the Ministry of Health. There were no restrictions on the right to use contraceptives, but access was limited in rural areas. The Malawi National Statistical Office (NSO) estimated 43.2 percent of married women of reproductive age used a modern method of contraception. The government provided free childbirth services, but their availability depended upon access to hospitals and other medical facilities in rural areas. The NSO estimated the maternal mortality rate was 634 deaths per 100,000 live births, and a woman's lifetime risk of maternal death was one in 29. AIDS and adolescent pregnancy both were factors in these high rates. The NSO estimated 29 percent of girls and young women ages 15 to 19 gave birth each year. Nurses and midwives were a critical component of prenatal and postnatal care due to a shortage of doctors. According to the NSO, skilled health-care providers assisted in 90 percent of births in 2015. There was only limited access to emergency obstetric care, however, particularly in rural areas.

Discrimination: By law women have the same legal status and rights as men and may not be discriminated against based on gender or marital status, including in the workplace. Women had significantly lower levels of literacy, education, and formal and nontraditional employment opportunities, as well as lower rates of access to resources for farming.

Women often had less access to legal and financial assistance, and widows often were victims of discriminatory and illegal inheritance practices in which most of an estate was taken by the deceased husband's family.

Women usually were at a disadvantage in marriage, family, and property rights; however, awareness of women's legal rights continued to increase. Households headed by women were predominately in the lowest quarter of income distribution. More than half--52 percent--of full-time farmers were women, but they had limited access to agricultural extension services, training, and credit.

The law provides for a minimum level of child support, widows' rights, and maternity leave; however, only women employed in the formal sector knew their rights and had access to the legal system, and thus benefited from these legal protections.

The government addressed women's concerns through the Ministry of Gender, Children, Disability, and Social Welfare.

Children

Birth Registration: Citizenship may be derived from birth within the country or abroad to at least one Malawian parent "of African race." According to the most recent population census (2008), 16.6 percent of children under age 18 had a birth certificate. Compulsory universal birth registration, enacted in 2012, became effective in August 2015, and four hospitals initiated electronic birth registration and issuance of legal birth certificates. There were no reports of discrimination or denial of services due to lack of birth registration.

Education: The government provided tuition-free primary education for all children. Education for children under age 18 is compulsory. Families were responsible for paying book fees and purchasing uniforms. Students from poor families had access to a public book fund. Many girls, especially in rural areas, were unable to complete primary education or transition to secondary education due to poverty, inaccessibility of schools or lack of capacity in schools, early and forced marriage, adolescent pregnancy, and cultural factors such as girls having a greater burden than boys of household responsibilities and parental preference to educate boys. Consequently they were at a serious disadvantage in finding employment. The *2015-16 Demographic and Health Survey* (DHS) found that 5 percent of men and 12 percent of women had no formal education.

Child Abuse: Child abuse remained a serious problem. The press regularly reported cases of sexual abuse of children, including arrests for rape, incest, sodomy, and defilement. The *2014 Violence Against Children Survey* found that one in five women and one in seven men ages 18 to 24 experienced at least one incident of sexual abuse prior to age 18. Two in five women and two in three men ages 18 to 24 experienced physical violence prior to age 18. Less than a quarter of individuals ages 18 to 24 knew of a place to seek help.

The law prohibits subjecting a child to any social or customary practice that is harmful to health or general development. Prohibited practices included child trafficking, forced labor, early and forced marriage or betrothal, and use of children as security for loans or other debts.

Ministry of Gender, Children, Disability, and Social Welfare activities to enhance protection and support of child victims included reuniting rescued victims of child labor with their parents and operating shelters for vulnerable children.

Early and Forced Marriage: The Marriage, Divorce, and Family Relations Act sets the minimum age for marriage at 18, but the constitution allows marriage at age 15 with parental consent. According to the UN Children's Fund *State of the World's Children 2016* report, 9 percent of girls and women ages 15 to 49 were first married or in a union before age 15, and 46 percent were married or in a union before age 18. The minimum marital age was not widely enforced, and civic education on early marriage was carried out mainly by NGOs. Some traditional leaders annulled early marriages and returned the girls involved to school.

Reflecting strong political will, ending child marriage was one of the three commitments made by the president as a global champion of the UN Entity for Gender Equality and the Empowerment of Women 2016 "He for She" campaign and a high priority of the Ministry of Gender, Children, Disability, and Social Welfare.

<u>Female Genital Mutilation/Cutting</u>: See information for girls under age 18 in women's section above.

<u>Sexual Exploitation of Children</u>: The law forbids engaging in sexual activity with children under age 16 and stipulates penalties for conviction of 14 to 21 years in prison. The law further prohibits "indecent practice" in the presence of or with a child, with offenders liable to imprisonment of up to 14 years.

The law prohibits child pornography and using a child for public entertainment of an immoral or harmful nature. The maximum penalty for conviction of engaging in child pornography is 14 years in prison, while those found guilty of procuring a child for public entertainment are liable to a fine of 100,000 MWK ($138) and imprisonment of seven years. The law was not effectively enforced.

The widespread belief that children were unlikely to be HIV-positive and that sexual intercourse with virgins could cleanse an individual of sexually transmitted diseases, including HIV/AIDS, contributed to the widespread sexual exploitation of minors. The *2014 Violence Against Children Survey* reported one in five women ages 18 to 24 experienced sexual violence before age 18. The average age for the first incident of sexual abuse was under 14 for both genders. More than a third of women ages 18 to 24 reported their first sexual intercourse was rape.

The trafficking of children for sexual purposes was a problem, and child prostitution for survival at the behest of parents or without third-party involvement occurred. At local bars and rest houses, owners coerced girls as young as age 12 to have sex with customers in exchange for room and board.

<u>Displaced Children</u>: The 2010 DHS found that 19 percent of children under age 18 were not living with either biological parent and that 17 percent were orphaned or vulnerable due to extended parental illness or death, including an estimated

650,000 orphaned because of AIDS. Extended family members normally cared for such children and other orphans.

International Child Abductions: The country is not a party to the 1980 Hague Convention on the Civil Aspects of International Child Abduction. See the Department of State's *Annual Report on International Parental Child Abduction* at travel.state.gov/content/childabduction/en/legal/compliance.html.

Anti-Semitism

The Jewish community was very small, and there were no known reports of anti-Semitic acts.

Trafficking in Persons

See the Department of State's *Trafficking in Persons Report* at www.state.gov/j/tip/rls/tiprpt/.

Persons with Disabilities

The Disability Act prohibits discrimination in education, health care, the judicial system, social services, the workplace, housing, political life, and cultural and sporting activities for persons with disabilities, defined as a long-term physical, mental, intellectual, or sensory impairment. The law prohibits discrimination against persons with disabilities in political and public life and calls for the government to take measures to provide access for them to transportation, information, and communication services. The law provides for the establishment of a disability trust fund to support persons with disabilities, including with regard to access to public facilities, both governmental and private.

Societal stigma related to disability and the lack of accessibility to public buildings and transportation had a negative impact on the ability of persons with disabilities to obtain services and obtain and maintain employment.

Accommodations for persons with disabilities were not among the government's priorities. Although the Disability Act took effect in 2013, the government had yet to adopt standards and plans for its enforcement and implementation. The Ministry of Gender, Children, Disability, and Social Welfare is responsible for protecting the rights of persons with disabilities, but inadequate resources precluded it from doing so.

There were public and privately supported schools and training centers that assisted persons with disabilities. In 2015 a disability advocacy group noted unlawful discrimination against women and children with disabilities was more prevalent in rural areas and that it received several reports of children with disabilities having to leave school because of inadequate accommodations.

As of September the MHRC reported receiving seven complaints related to disability rights and concluded investigations into three of them. The complaints regarded the insufficient availability of wheelchairs, inadequate access to schooling for children with disabilities, and the unavailability of sunscreen at a health facility for an individual with albinism.

Acts of Violence, Discrimination, and Other Abuses Based on Sexual Orientation and Gender Identity

LGBTI persons are denied by law and practice basic civil, political, social, and economic rights. Consensual same-sex sexual activity is illegal and punishable if convicted by up to 14 years in prison, including hard labor. The penal code outlaws "unnatural offenses" and "indecent practices between males." In 2014, however, Solicitor General Janet Banda told the UN Human Rights Commission the government would not enforce these laws. In December 2015 Minister of Justice Samuel Tembenu reaffirmed the moratorium on the enforcement of laws criminalizing consensual same-sex sexual activity and continued the moratorium during the year.

In 2013 the High Court invited friend-of-the-court submissions on the constitutionality of laws against "unnatural offenses" and "indecent practices between males." It received arguments both for and against the laws' constitutionality, with most of the arguments being in opposition. The attorney general filed a motion with the Supreme Court objecting to the process on the basis that the chief justice must certify constitutional questions and obtained an order in 2014 suspending the proceedings. On August 2, the attorney general withdrew the government's objection to the process, thus allowing the constitutional review to resume. As a result a panel of no fewer than three High Court judges was planned to conduct the review, but no date had been set by year's end.

Same-sex sexual activity may also be prosecuted as "conduct likely to cause a breach of the peace." A 2011 amendment to the penal code established penalties for consensual same-sex sexual activity between women, setting a maximum prison term for conviction of five years.

From January to October, the Center for Development of People documented 19 instances of abuse based on sexual orientation and gender identity. The nature of the abuses fell into three broad categories: stigma, harassment, and violence. *The Weekend Nation* newspaper published a weekly column entitled "Sexual Minority Forum" written by the leaders of human rights NGOs to shed light on conditions affecting LGBTI persons and their rights.

HIV and AIDS Social Stigma

Societal discrimination against persons with HIV/AIDS remained a problem, especially in rural areas. Many individuals preferred to keep silent regarding their health conditions rather than seek help and risk being ostracized. Campaigns by the government and NGOs to combat the stigma had some success. The National AIDS Commission maintained that discrimination was a problem in both the public and private sectors.

The *2012 People Living with HIV Stigma Index for Malawi* indicated that of 2,272 persons with HIV interviewed, significant percentages reported having been verbally insulted/harassed/threatened (35.1 percent) and excluded from social gatherings (33.7 percent).

Other Societal Violence or Discrimination

Mobs and local citizens sometimes engaged in vigilante attacks, at times killing persons suspected of crimes such as theft.

There were several attacks against persons with albinism driven by the demand for body parts for witchcraft rituals in neighboring Tanzania. Religious, traditional, civil society, and political leaders, including the president, publicly denounced the attacks. The government launched a public awareness campaign and conducted training of police, prosecutors, and judges in border districts to counter the trend.

Section 7. Worker Rights

a. Freedom of Association and the Right to Collective Bargaining

The law allows workers, except for military personnel and police, to form and join trade unions of their choice without previous authorization or excessive requirements. Unions must register with the Registrar of Trade Unions and Employers' Organizations in the Ministry of Labor. The law places some restrictions on the right to collectively bargain, including requirements of prior authorization by authorities, and bargaining status. The law provides for unions to conduct their activities without government interference. The law also prohibits antiunion discrimination and provides for remedial measures in cases of dismissal for union activity. The law does not specifically prohibit retaliation against strikers or actions against unions that are not registered.

Workers in the formal sector have the right to organize and bargain collectively. The law requires that at least 20 percent of employees (excluding senior managerial staff) must belong to a union before it may engage in collective bargaining at the enterprise (factory) level, and at least 15 percent of employees must be union members for collective bargaining at the sector (industry) level. The law provides for the establishment of industrial councils in the absence of collective agreements for sector-level bargaining. Industrial council functions include wage negotiation, dispute resolution, and industry-specific labor policy development. The law allows members of a registered union to strike or go through a formal mediation process overseen by the Ministry of Labor. A strike may take place only after a lengthy settlement procedure set out in the Labor Relations Act has failed. The law also requires the labor minister to apply to the Industrial Relations Court to determine whether a particular strike involves an "essential service," the interruption of which would endanger the life, health, or personal safety of part of the population. The law does not provide a specific list of essential services. Members of a registered union in essential services have only a limited right to strike. There are no special laws or exemptions from regular labor laws in export processing zones. The law does not apply to the vast majority of workers who are in the informal sectors.

The government did not effectively enforce applicable laws. As was true of all cases entering the justice system, choices relating to the allocation of limited resources and lack of capacity resulted in delays of some labor cases. Penalties for violations were insufficient to deter violations, mainly consisting of small fines of 1,000 MWK to 50,000 MWK ($1.39 to $69). Provisions exist for custodial punishment of up to two years in prison, but none was reported.

Freedom of association and the right to collective bargaining were adequately respected for those in the formal sector. The law requires that unions must be registered, and registration was granted routinely. Union membership among workers was low due to the small percentage of the workforce in the formal sector and a lack of awareness of worker rights.

Employers, labor unions, and the government lacked sufficient knowledge of their roles in labor relations and disputes. In general the government respected the right to collective bargaining.

Arbitration rulings were legally enforceable; however, the Industrial Relations Court did not monitor cases or adequately enforce the laws.

Informal sector workers organized in the Malawi Union for the Informal Sector (MUFIS), which is affiliated with the Malawi Congress of Trade Unions. MUFIS worked with district councils to address issues affecting informal workers due in part to a Ministry of Labor decision that MUFIS did not have sufficient standing to bargain collectively with employers. According to the *2013 Malawi Labour Force Survey*, of the 7.8 million persons in the working population, 88.7 percent were in the informal sector.

b. Prohibition of Forced or Compulsory Labor

The law prohibits all forms of forced or compulsory labor. Forced labor is punishable by a maximum fine of 10,000 MWK ($13.83) or two years' imprisonment. The government did not effectively enforce applicable laws.

Children were subjected to domestic servitude and other forms of forced labor, including cattle herding; bonded labor on plantations, particularly on tobacco farms; and menial work in small businesses. Punishments were limited to modest fines that did not deter labor violations.

Also see the Department of State's *Trafficking in Persons Report* at www.state.gov/j/tip/rls/tiprpt/.

c. Prohibition of Child Labor and Minimum Age for Employment

The law sets the minimum age for employment at 14, and children between the ages 14 and 18 may not work in hazardous jobs or jobs that interfere with their education. The prohibition of child labor does not apply to work done in homes, vocational technical schools, or other training institutions. The law prohibits child trafficking, including labor exploitation and the forced labor of children for the income of a parent or guardian. The Employment Act provides a list of hazardous work for children and specifies a maximum fine of 20,000 MWK ($27.66) or five years' imprisonment for violations. The law, however, was not effectively enforced due to lack of resources and staffing. Penalties and enforcement were insufficient to deter offenders.

Police and Ministry of Labor officials were responsible for enforcing child labor laws and policies. Labor inspectors do not have law enforcement authority and must enlist police to pursue violators.

The Ministry of Labor carried out inspections, focused mainly on agricultural estates, but enforcement by police and ministry inspectors of child labor laws was minimal. By its own admission, the government made little progress to implement its 2010-16 National Action Plan on Child Labor. Most public education activities were carried out by tobacco companies--tobacco is the country's largest export-- and NGOs.

Child labor remained a serious and widespread problem. The NSO 2014 *Malawi Millennium Development Goal Endline Survey* found that almost 40 percent of children ages five to 17 were engaged in some form of child labor. Child labor was prevalent on tobacco farms, subsistence farms, and in domestic service. Many boys worked as vendors, and young girls in urban areas often worked outside of their families as domestic servants, receiving low or no wages.

Also see the Department of Labor's *Findings on the Worst Forms of Child Labor* at www.dol.gov/ilab/reports/child-labor/findings/.

d. Discrimination with Respect to Employment and Occupation

The employment law prohibits discrimination against any employee or prospective employee on the grounds of race, color, sex, language, religion, political or other opinion, nationality, ethnic or social origin, disability, property, birth, marital or other status, family responsibilities or HIV/AIDS and other communicable disease status, but the government in general did not effectively enforce the law.

Discrimination in employment and occupation occurred with respect to gender and disability (see section 6). Despite the law against discrimination based on gender or marital status, discrimination against women was pervasive, and women did not have opportunities equal to those available to men. Women had significantly lower levels of literacy, education, and formal and nontraditional employment opportunities. Few women participated in the limited formal labor market, and those that did represented only a very small portion of managerial and administrative staff. Households headed by women were overrepresented in the lowest quarter of income distribution.

Migrant workers are entitled to the same legal protections, wages, and working conditions as citizens if they comply with immigration laws. Those persons not in compliance are subject to deportation.

e. Acceptable Conditions of Work

The minister of labor sets the minimum wage rate based on recommendations of the Tripartite Wage Advisory Board, which is composed of representatives of labor, government, and employers. The minimum wage was 688 MWK ($0.95) per day as of October 2015. The *2014 Integrated Household Survey* estimated 50.7 percent of citizens lived below the poverty line. There was no exception to the requirement of paying the minimum wage for foreign or migrant workers.

The Ministry of Labor lacked the capacity to enforce the minimum wage effectively. Official minimum wages apply only to the formal sector and thus did not apply to most citizens, who earned their livelihood outside the formal wage sector. Wage earners often supplemented their incomes through farming activities. No government programs provided social protections for workers in the informal economy.

The maximum legal workweek is 48 hours, with a mandatory weekly 24-hour rest period. The law requires payment for overtime work and prohibits compulsory overtime. The workweek standards were not effectively enforced, and employers frequently violated statutory time restrictions. The Ministry of Labor's enforcement of health and safety standards was also poor. The law specifies a maximum fine of 20,000 MWK ($27.66) or five years' imprisonment for violations. The fines were not sufficient to deter offenders and there have never been reports of jail terms.

The law includes extensive occupational health and safety standards. The Ministry of Labor houses a Directorate of Occupational Safety and Health. The government did not effectively enforce the law. Workers, particularly in industrial jobs, often worked without basic safety clothing and equipment. In tobacco fields workers harvesting leaves generally did not were protective clothing; workers absorbed up to 54 milligrams of dissolved nicotine daily through their skin, the equivalent of 50 cigarettes. Thousands of child tobacco workers suffered from nicotine poisoning. These children often worked 12-hour days, frequently for little or no pay.

Workers have the right to remove themselves from dangerous work situations without jeopardy to continued employment. Workers dismissed for filing complaints regarding workplace conditions have the right to file a complaint at the labor office or sue the employer for wrongful dismissal; however, due to ignorance of such rights and high levels of unemployment, workers were unlikely to exercise these rights. Additionally, authorities did not effectively protect employees in this situation.